Wisdom Gone Wrong

CHRISTINE HARE

Author's Tranquility Press
ATLANTA, GEORGIA

Copyright © 2024 by Christine Hare

All rights reserved. No part of this publication may be reproduced, distributed or transmitted in any form or by any means, including photocopying, recording, or other electronic or mechanical methods, without the prior written permission of the publisher, except in the case of brief quotations embodied in critical reviews and certain other noncommercial uses permitted by copyright law. For permission requests, write to the publisher, addressed "Attention: Permissions Coordinator," at the address below.

Christine Hare/Author's Tranquility Press
3900 N Commerce Dr. Suite 300 #1255
Atlanta, GA 30344
www.authorstranquilitypress.com

Ordering Information:
Quantity sales. Special discounts are available on quantity purchases by corporations, associations, and others. For details, contact the "Special Sales Department" at the address above.

Wisdom Gone Wrong/Christine Hare
Paperback: 978-1-964362-88-5
eBook: 978-1-964037-68-4

Contents

The Old Man and the Spider 1
Ray and the Rat Race 2
Bart the Fart... 3
Mary's Surprise 4
Smith and the Hot Dish.. 5
Forgetful Fred 6
Sleepless Kay 7
Sam, the party Ham 8
Brady, the Lady-Charmer... 9
Fisherman Jim.. 10
Helen's Hearing 11
Sleep-Talking Pete 12
Cheap Steve 13
Late Kate.. 14
Know It All Paul 15
LuAnn's Perfect Party Plan... 16
Scott's Big Dreams 17
The Junkyard Car 18
Thoughtless Gill... 19
Self-Centered Ralph 20
Jack and the Sparrow.. 21
Gabby Gail 22
Sexy Mabel... 23
Halfway Paul.. 24
Blue Sue... 25
Chad's Crush 26

The Old Man and the Spider

A grumpy old man tried to kill a spider on the wall.
He said, "Spiders should not live at all!"

He was surprised when the spider replied,
"Sir, you're going to wish that you were dead when I jump in your hair
and make a permanent home in your head!"

The moral of the story simply is this:
If you kill a spider, you'd better not miss!

Ray and the Rat Race

Here is a tale of a fellow named Ray. He lived a hectic life;
his boss wanted everything done by yesterday.

Driving around one Saturday, he picked up a lost dog along the way.
Ray's nonexistent being became alive as the exhausted
pooch curled up at his side.
The little dog became a part of Ray's heart; both of them
enjoyed fun walks in the park.
Together, they brought joy to each other. It put a smile on Ray's face,
His new furry friend helped him slow down the pace.

Our busy lives make us feel beat, find relief,
"Take time to smell the flowers before you find yourself six feet
underneath!"

Bart the Fart

There was a man called "Party Bart" with a special art for a fart.
It was a part of his ingenious plan.

He laid a fart really loud; the smell quickly emptied out a crowd.
Then by the food in an empty place, he was first in line to feed his face.

If you really want to keep and not chase away friends,
just use a smile, but not your rear end!

Mary's Surprise

Mary's new husband was sweet, loving, and kind,
but like an unopened book. She wondered what else she would find.

Mary got quite a surprise, tears in her eyes,
when he took off his shoes and the smell knocked her off her feet.
They worked on a cure—it was quite a relief!

It's been said, "You can't tell a book by its cover,"
until you take the time to look underneath!

Smith and the Hot Dish

There once was a man called Smith, who wished
he could meet a very hot dish,
When his dream came alive, Smith was a very happy guy.

He loved her and tried to give her all that she asked,
dreaming of his honeymoon.
But all too soon, the dish ran off with a rich man
holding a silver spoon.

All I have to say is this: Be careful when you make a wish.
Prepare words carefully when you do, because your
wish may come true!

Forgetful Fred

When Fred married Jenny, he left his mind behind.
Twenty years later he is still forgetful, deaf, dumb, and blind.

Recently, Fred remembered something from what
Jenny said, and had done:
The reason they married is because "two heads are better than one."

Here's a word to the wise: When most men get married,
their minds master a particular quirk—
pretend to forget to get out of housework!

Sleepless Kay

There once was a woman named Kay, who was tired every day.
At night she couldn't sleep or even count sheep.
Her husband's terrible snoring drove them away.

She tried to explain to Ted, who scoffed, denied it, and said,
"You're making this all up in your head."
Kay's eyes bugged out, and her face turned red.
She threw his pillow in the spare room, into Ted's permanent bed!

"When you make your bed you lie in it." This story
proves that it's true.
Men, watch out what you say because this could happen to you!

Sam, the party Ham

I once knew a man named Sam. In a group he was a quite ham.
He told uncomfortable stories and thought he was funny,
also embarrassing his poor wife, Ann.

At one special party he felt extra hearty, saying something outrageous
about the wrong guy. Sam was surprised about the reprise—
a black eye was not part of his plan!

For people like Sam, here's a word to the wise.
Before telling a story make sure you know your friends well, and
don't kid around with someone three times your size!

Brady, the Lady-Charmer

A handsome young man named Brady was quite
a charmer with the ladies.
He puffed out his chest and said, "I'm the best." Brady
dated many women
with beautiful looks. He rated them all in his little black book.

His girlfriends found out all in good time. To them this was not fine.
Together they met and decided his fate. Brady was
brought to the park,
where the women confronted him, speaking their minds.
Suddenly, Brady was not such a brave heart!

When life lets you down and there is a good reason,
"Don't get mad, get even!"

Fisherman Jim

I once had a friend named Jim. He loved to fish but had
a fear of the water,
and never learned how to swim. Living near the ocean,
he fished off the end of a long wooden pier.

Suddenly, a big fish tugged at his line. Jim fought back, saying,
"This one is mine."
But the fish proved stronger and it pulled him in.
He remembered too late the term "Sink or swim!"

When you're near deep water it's not good to test fate—
you just might fall in and become fish bait!

Helen's Hearing

Helen was sweet but enduring and didn't believe
that she was hard of hearing.
It was dismaying to get into conversations
without a clear thought of what they were saying.

One day in a large crowd someone asked Helen if she knew Fred.
She got mad and answered back loudly, "What do you mean by that?
Do I look dead!"
When the story got back to what she had said, Helen felt
embarrassed and dumb.
The very next day she had a hearing test done!

If you think all people speak low, and mumble,
then your social life will certainly crumble!

Sleep-Talking Pete

Pete was unique. Out of guilt, he talked in his sleep.
His wife, a light sleeper, heard everything, which got him into
trouble deeper.

One night she taped him to prove it was fact.
This time he mumbled about
not going to some boring show that she wanted to see,
because of a special sports activity. When Pete heard what he had said
his face turned red, and he was at a loss for words.

When you practice to deceive, they'll know,
and you will get what's coming.
Remember, "You reap what you sow!"

Cheap Steve

Steve and his wife brought home decent pay at the end of each week,
but Steve was cheap and hated to spend any
He did not buy underwear,
socks, or shoes for his feet. His favorite old clothes
were worn and beat.
The roof leaked, but he would not spare the funds
to get the job done.

One spring morning it thundered and poured hard all day.
It was the worst that it had ever been. Steve heard a loud noise.
Then the ceiling fell in, which also ruined the carpet and floor.
It cost him three times more to have it fixed than
it would have before!

"A penny saved is a penny earned" shows values, I know,
but you can't take it with you when it's your time to go!

Late Kate

Kate moved at a slow pace and thought nothing of being
fashionably late.
She left no shame when making life crazy for people at work
or meeting friends because she was never on time.

One night she was thirty minutes late for her dinner date
With her boyfriend, Kyle.
He decided not to wait and left a message with the waiter.
When Kate finally arrived, reading the note, she went home and
cried. It said,
"I'm sorry you didn't show up tonight. I was going to propose and
make you my wife.
I'm not coming back. Have a good life"

Kate's philosophy, "Better late than never." did not pay!

Know It All Paul

Paul pretended that he knew it all. To make himself look better
he purposely made others feel small. On the job he
gloated and boasted
that he was going to speak at the work conference next week.

Meeting his associates in another town, Paul was the
only one who did not
write the directions down. Lost! Paul's heart began to race,
but he had too much pride to stop and ask directions to the place.
In the end he was late, and going home was his only fate.
To save face with others the next day he lied and said,
"I had car trouble along the way."

Feeling insecure inside is a human flaw. There are positive choices
to get it together, but "Pride goeth before a fall."

LuAnn's Perfect Party Plan

LuAnn tried to create the perfect birthday party
for her young son, Nate.
When the hard work was done, having everything in its right place
put a happy smile on her face.

All was fine until the party guests arrived.
Then everything went insane.
Bored with the games, the kids ran all over the place.
LuAnn went crazy. It was all she could take.
To quit them down and slow down their pace,
she sat them all the table, shouting, "Let them eat cake!"

When things fail to go perfect, don't have a cow.
Perhaps plan B will work better somehow!

Scott's Big Dreams

Scott had big plans for his future, dreaming ahead
toward something rewarding,
perhaps a job that was enjoyable. He walked around
with his head in the clouds,
wishing his life away, hoping his ship would
come in some day.

There were many things Scott wanted to try.
His negative thought said
it would not work, and he would come up dry.
It the end he was unhappy,
settling for less when he could have strived to have the best.

Don't sit around waiting for your ship to come in.
Reach for the stars,
Because a rowboat won't get you very far!

The Junkyard Car

One day, Mark's dad bought home a junky old car.
Mark was stunned
and said, "This car looks beat up, and barely runs."
His father replied, "We're going to rebuild it, wait until it's done."
All extra nickels and dimes were put to use fixing the
car in their spare time.

Many hard-working hours were spent recovering the seats.
On the outside
they rebuilt the engine, and fixed all the dents.
Carefully, the car was given
a shiny silver coat of paint, saving for the last, new tires
and fancy hub caps.
Staring at the car they felt proud inside, an adventure
That filled them with pride.

Don't let problems stand in your way. "When life gives you lemons,
make lemonade!"

Thoughtless Gill

When Beth married Gill, she did not realize that he had
Little insight of women.
When birthdays and other occasions came near, she would
give him hints
which he did not hear. It wasn't a thrill to open a gift
such as a tool set, lawn mower, or grill.

One Christmas as the last straw, Beth bought a nightgown,
sexy underwear,
and a bra. She wrapped it all up and marked it, to Gill. When he
opened the boxes
his eyes could not believe and he said, "What am I supposed to
do with these!"
Beth returned with, "I'm sorry that you did not get you wish.
I'll trade you the drill that you gave me, and we can switch!"

When a woman hints at a gift, listen up before it turns into this!

Self-Centered Ralph

I knew of a man called Ralph. He was very self-centered
and thought of nobody else.
He did not perceive other person's problems or needs.

One day—he was driving too fast—Ralph's car swerved and careened
into a ditch, hardly to be seen.
He was injured. It was rainy and cold. Ralph heard the scars above
and could barely
see them go by. Lots of hours passed. Only two persons looked
down. Ralph was upset
that they did not stop. He had plenty of time to think about how he
had treated others,
and his heart began to sink. He vowed to change,
realizing that he was wrong,
and was very grateful when help finally came along!

The saying "Do unto others as you would have others do unto you"
stand on the solid ground, Remember, "What goes around comes
around!"

Jack and the Sparrow

While washing his car in the warm morning breeze
Jack sprayed water
on a noisy sparrow perched on a branch, up in a tree.
Working hard at a fast pace, Jack didn't realize
there were many others
gathering in the same place.

The angry birds decided to wait till Jack finished, to seal his fate.
When the shiny, waxed car gleamed in the noon sun,
Jack was stunned
when they dive-bombed and pooped on his car, one by one!

"Birds of a feather flock together," so don't be dumb.
When you upset one bird you'll upset the other ones!

Gabby Gail

This is a story about Gail, who wanted to be everyone's pal.
Meeting people, she would talk them off their feet,
not giving them a single chance to speak.

When anyone tried to tell Gail something important, she didn't hear;
not a single word entered her ears. Insecure,
Gail could not understand
why she often missed out on special events and plans.

The saying goes "It's better to be seen and not heard." This is sometimes true.
Try to smile, listen, and observe. You will learn what's new
plus the feeling of others, drawing friends closer to you!

Sexy Mabel

Mabel, a spunky spring chicken, really liked a handsome senior,
vowing to get him to please her. She smiled and
winked when Charlie
passed by every day, but he just grumbled and looked away.

Not giving up, Mabel wore something sexy to bingo each week.
Soon he was turning his head to peek. She did funny things
to make him laugh.
Charlie finally broke down and made a pass.
Together as a couple, they shared happiness that would last.

It goes to show that love and laughter are important,
and still the rage.
No matter what people may say, you can teach an old dog new tricks.
It's all in the mind, not in the age!

Halfway Paul

Young married Paul cooked a surprise dinner for his wife, Kate,
coming home from work late. Smiling, she thanked
him, saying it was great,
giving him kisses.

Afterwards, Kate was in awe when she saw a pile of pots and pans in
the sink, and food splattered on the stove and the wall. She asked
Paul if he had forgotten
it all? "No," he replied, "when I cooked at home
my mother would clean."
Kate's eyes bugged out. With an angry look on her face,
she just pointed.
To honor her wishes Paul ran into the kitchen, washing the wall and
the dishes!

If you can't finish the job don't start the mission. Take it from Paul:
"If you can't stand the heat, stay out of the kitchen!"

Blue Sue

I once knew a woman named Sue, who adored her husband and child
but often felt blue. She longed to be like the neighbors next door;
they had money, vacations, and more. Sue and her husband always
worked hard on the job, or at home with the chores and the yard.

One afternoon on a walk in the park her daughter saw something
and said a funny remark. Sue was surprised, laughing so hard
she had tears in her eyes. Looking back she recalled other fun times
like at the beach, and the zoo. Suddenly, she realized that
happiness does not
have to be on a grand scale but that "good things come in a small
packages," too.

The big things in life may only be few. It's the little things that count,
like the joy of family and friends around you!

Chad's Crush

Chad had a crush on the most beautiful girl in school.
He tried to look
and act cool in her direction, but she never paid any attention.

One Saturday he received a call she wanted a date,
and to meet him at a
special place to eat in the mall. With the unbelievable news
Chad dressed up
in his best duds and shoes. The sweet smell of April was in the air—
its too bad he did not pick up on the clues. When Chad
arrived, his friends
jumped out and said, "Surprise, April fool." At the first he was mad
but then had to laugh because he had played jokes
on them in the past.

When someone tells you something, incredibly certain,
think it through.
"If it sounds too good to be true, it probably is!"

www.ingramcontent.com/pod-product-compliance
Lightning Source LLC
LaVergne TN
LVHW040204080526
838202LV00042B/3313